From a Fidgety Mind

lewis turner

BookLeaf
Publishing

India | USA | UK

Presentation by *BookLeaf Publishing*

Web: www.bookleafpub.com

E-mail: info@bookleafpub.com

ISBN: 9789358738131

First edition 2023

For my Darling wife Mrs Fiona Turner, I could write till my dying day telling endless different poems and stories and no words strung together would ever be as beautiful as my bear. xx

ACKNOWLEDGEMENT

I would like to acknowledge the following people: my family and friends for giving me everything in life, for helping me shape a conscience that can feel and think this way, some of the poems can be a little dark and glum but all of that is constantly outshined by your love and support, to my colleagues in work who have supported me with this and read my work when they're trying to just have a cuppa tea on a break, A special mention to Debbie Oddie for the idea on what to call the book, she said after I would have a panic attack in work it looks like your mind and hands would just fidget, so that's where the title comes from.

PREFACE

Like everyone in life, we have moments in our days where we feel a certain way, lost, lonely, scared, anxious or depressed; a lot of these poems came into my head when times were quiet when it was just me and my thoughts whilst I was struggling with depression or severe anxiety attacks, which I wouldn't wish on anyone. If anyone reads this and they are struggling, there is help out there and I hope just one of these poems connected with you in some way. I slowly made it out of my depression and anxiety and I continued to write for fun and to relax. My family says I have a gift; I'm unsure about that but if it is my gift to write poems that connect then I want to share that as far and wide as I can.

My four-legged friend

My four-legged friend never fails to make me smile, Always happy to see me even if I have only been away a wee while.

Woken up first thing out to the garden they go, They won't hang around long if the weather is rain or snow, Back in the house to see what's in the bowl, the food is always nice but a sausage is the ultimate goal.

Off to the park to run around and go nuts, stopping to sniff every plant and tree no ifs or buts. Time to head home, they look with that look as if to say five minutes longer,
Ok fine I guess I need to be stronger.

The end of the day they sit on your lap, comfy, safe it's time for a nap, off to bed the day is at an end, I can't wait for tomorrow with my four-legged friend.

For the grandparents

A grandparent is special in every kind of way,
from the things they do, to the past phrases
they say, Always excited to take your call and
add another photo, pride of place on their
wall

They may not fully understand the things of
today, it may have been different for them
growing up in a roundabout way.

They've been around longer with a lifetime of
knowledge and advice for you to take, forever
happy to see you, share a cuppa tea and a fine
slice of cake.

All grandparents are different like yours from
mine, some are still with us, others are stars
that shine.

If you have the chance hug them and tell
them you love them too and if you can't I'm
sorry but always remember their spirit and
love is forever with you.

Fireworks against the stars

Technology brings us closer together yet we are drifting apart, useful and useless info makes us colder at heart.

A virtual life lived, checked upon throughout the day, another thought, opinion a click and send away.

Take my phone away and you are taking part of me, like a man with no sight unable to see. Back in my hand I can't let go, what's the latest trends and gossip I just have to know.

I am not a robot just confirming for the time being, we can see it all in the world without really seeing.

Some get tired realising technology has us all, like fireworks against the stars missing the real beauty behind it all.

Broken Bridges

Standing at our final crossing, holding your toll token, unable to cross our bridge that lies broken, it takes a lot of time and love to rebuild, but looking at the damage I'm just not that skilled.

Another way forward must be ahead, one without you onwards alone instead, you can't come now, my decision is made. The debt on this damage is just being paid, in my memories you can stay with the past. A painful journey I'm sure to outlast.

Life is one big journey, paths can be clear and others can be blocked, some get smooth sailing other boats are rocked, for me it's never easy it's always so rough, I thought our time together would be a little less tough.

Every obstruction and every path's sharp bend
Never tackled alone as long as I have one friend, onwards believing my journey will come right in the end.

Another lonely train of thought

Restless on a journey into my thoughts.
Carriages of broken dreams and
forget-me-nots.

It's free to ride but you will pay in the end
this journey's for one you can't take a friend.

seats a plenty but there's only just me
looking out the windows only darkness to see.

I want to get off but the train picks up pace
faster to my sorrow it's like losing a race.

My train screeches to a halt no time to think.
I will surely finish up this journey with
another lonely drink.

A world of balloons

My world is a balloon, lifted by your air,
bouncing, fragile and carefree so long as you
are there.

Connected to you through a big piece of
string, tied round your finger your shiny
wedding ring.

Making you happy and keeping me safe high
from harm, everywhere together your smile
drives my charm.

Here for you always a love never to deflate
nor drop, a special kind of balloon on you can
pop.

<u>*The mirror before the start*</u>

I will look in the mirror and stare into my
eyes. Trying to look deeper, a search for what
my smile can't disguise.

Something just feels different not as in touch
or taste, something is missing that can't be
replaced. Uncaring if it's normal, only that
it's OK, I'll move on as best I can, hope leads
the way.

I'm still me and I have made it this far, what's
one more lesson a wound turned into a scar.
We never forget and that's fine too.
A focus turned to good times, friends and
family see me through.

Another day ahead I will go at my own pace,
taking time out slowly if needed, I'm in no
one's race.

Hospital Clock

The hospital clock is something no one wants
to see,
people wishing it would speed up so they can
go home free,
others want it slowed down and the world to
leave them be.

They say time flies when you're having fun
but nothing flies here,
nurses do their best to ease minds and spread
cheer.
Visiting time a spark in the grey an
undisputed highlight in everyone's day.

Another day done a chance to sit back and
take stock.
All forever under the eye of that damn
hospital clock tick tock tick tock.

<u>A time to be Kind</u>

Do you feel accomplished in your day? Have
you used your time wisely? is what I mean to
say.
You only get one chance at today's date,
in 24 hours it's gone no rebate.

I am not judging please don't hate, we only
get a limited time as we slowly close life's
gate.

How you spend your time is up to you. I want
to make you stop and pause, think things
through. Were you kind to another, or did
you not even bother?

Kindness is a gift that is free to give, but
sometimes we just want to get on with our
own lives we have to live. It's not always easy
to think of others, the should, would, could
thoughts come out, as we crawl under the
duvet covers.

Another chance tomorrow, maybe a well wish
or two, could certainly help others when they
feel blue. If everyone was courteous, kind and

polite, I'm sure the world would sleep easier at night.

There are 24 hours on this limited day, a few seconds of kindness can go a long, long way.

Jewels and Fools

There is a jeweller at the end of the street
Run by the nicest family you'd ever want to
meet
But times are hard, we've had our last sob.
It's us against the world, tonight we rob.

We head out after dark, when the street is
dead
Just listen to me and keep the head. We won't
need much tools to grab these jewels, a
crowbar, gloves and of course a mask, just
stick with me I'll lead this task.

1:00 am sharp we put the window in, grab
what we can, those guys are insured it's a
win-win. I know a guy who can sell our loot,
we can't keep any, sell it all, get rid we need
every penny.

Keep a sharp eye as I break the glass, foot on
the peddle ready to hit the gas. The cost is
clear let's get this done, a little ahead of
schedule it's 12:51.

Up to the window, watches, necklaces and
rings it's ours to steal, not a care in the world
how the owners will feel, a quick glance at the
driver, gripping the steering wheel.

Crowbar ready it's time to swing, a crash, a
crack, an alarm starts to ring, not much time
and that cracked window still stands, time for
another swing I can't change plans. Bang and
shatter like a million stars glass everywhere
amongst the jewels, this was too easy, we've
taken them for fools.

Grab everything that shines and don't leave a
thing, not much time as the alarm continues
to ring. Hands on your head and down on the
ground, OK officer, my heart starts to pound.
I drop to the floor, as my driver speeds away,
the cops get me nicked he is the hero of the
day.

Down at the station they will ask who you are,
my accomplice, my partner driving the car.
There's me they've got and that might do, but
would I get a lighter sentence if they got you
too?

The Seagull

Sitting on a bench, staring at the sea.
A seagull wants my fries, I'm sure it's
followed me.
Never mind that look out there, the surfer in
the water catching some air, you wouldn't see
me do that even on a dare.

Kids running a plenty all around the sand,
loving parents behind them walking hand in
hand.
In the background the arcade music I hear.
"SQUAWK"
Mr seagull you're still here?

My fries are dwindling and so are your
chances
You hover around, your weird feet kinda
dances.
No more fries Mr Seagull, not a rogue one to
be seen,
Mine and your friendship would never have
been.

I dart forward, in hopes of scaring you away

You don't really move, tilting your head in a
mocking kinda way,
I jump forward and clap my hands, the
seagull won't move it just stands where it
stands.

Poe got his raven, you know the one that
screamed nevermore, and I got you a chip
beggar galore. You win Mr seagull I'm going
back to my car, A flying rodent that's all you
really are, when it comes to a nuisance you
raise the bar.

Arriving at my car, annoyed my peace was
shattered
Only to find on my windscreen bird poo
spattered.

<u>*A carer's Promise*</u>

Every day is different, none are the same
Encouraging independence is the name of the
game
First things first I can help you wake up, help
get you dressed, fix your hair and makeup.

A little bit of breakfast that's not too much
trouble one slice of toast or do you want
double?
Sometimes is hard to talk or say how you're
feeling this particular day. I'll take the time as
you convey, always patient that's just my way.

You may find it difficult what others do not,
I'm here to help no second thought, I can
make meals and help with a chore, yes even
the ones that can be a bit of a bore.

I can fill many roles throughout my shift,
cook, cleaner, nurse and more, I can even
plan trips if you want out the door. The day is
yours I can help you decide just here for
assistance just by your side.

Sure other jobs are easier, that's certainly
true, it's not about a wage more assisting you.

Through the Smoke

Searching through the grey smoke of my
memories,
trying to find burning memories of you,
The fire isn't as strong as it was and nor am I,
Hunting for the happy times refusing to let us
die.

Times change everything,
memories included are a little harder to
recall,
100% truth in my head, pride before the fall.

I will always find the fire, even when lost in
the smoke,
your smile your eyes more kindling for my
fire to stoke.

Forever burning, as is the world turning,
memories truly last a lifetime.

Detecting Fortune

The metal detector enthusiast sets off on his
day,
who knows what he could find something that
will pay?
Who knows what riches this field could yield.
deep in the dirt the soil so old please be nickel
silver or gold.

Scanning the ground, hoping to hear that
ping,
unsure of what it is yet it could be anything.
Most of the time it's nothing of note.
One day he will find his treasure then he will
gloat.

So far his find bag remains the same,
but patience and perseverance are the name
of this game.
A little red flag marking the area he has been,
so far fruitless his prize unseen.

Just a little more and then I will take a rest,
upwards and onwards a nice day my quest.
Deep beneath the earth and thicket ahead,
he hears the sound that stops him dead.

Deep into the ground, gently as he goes,
Who knows how long it's been there no one knows,
It glistens when he moves it's shiny in his palm.
This is it oh my god remain calm.
A golden coin, surely one of many,
He drops to his knees without a second thought,
Wait there's another one, Finally his jackpot!

A First Date

She sits at the bar, waiting on her date,
It's this moment that surely everyone must
hate.
Her hair and make up so meticulously done,
Who knows maybe this guy could finally be
the one.

She moves in her seat although trying to shift
her train of thought,
Here he comes, wow are those flowers he's
brought?
She stands up to greet him, wow he's really
tall,
We can be little and large no problem at all.

He leans in for a hug, yay that felt nice,
Just play it cool girl, like your drink with ice.
Hi I'm Fiona nice to finally meet you,
Hi I'm Lewis lovely to meet you too.

I brought you some flowers he sheepishly
says,
I take them from him (god I'll be smiling for
days)

We start to make small talk, he tells me he
loves dogs,
Wow he seems perfect, I think I've found a
winner,
We move over to our table and choose our
dinner.

His eyes are soft blue, I catch myself staring,
I tell him hurriedly I love the shirt he is
wearing,
His face turns red and he says thank you,
And by the way you look beautiful too.

The date's at an end and the dessert was
sweet,
But not as much as the man I went to meet.
He walks me to my taxi and asks to hold my
hand,
Yes of course that would be grand.

He kisses me on the cheek and tells me good
night,
He even says we can have a second date if you
like.

I try to play it down like it's no big deal,
But this has been amazing it can't be real,
I lean in and kiss him and say that would be
great,

And that dear reader is how I met my soul mate.

A Sideshow Tale

Lost on a path when I saw that huge black
tent.
A grey-faced man, with his moth-eaten suit
stood outside,
His smile crooked and broken but bursting
with pride,
The closer I got I couldn't look away,
He broke the silence when he started to say.

Gather round everyone, our moment of
intention has begun,
Please don't be scared it's just a little fun,
If you don't want to be here well it's too late
to run.

I can paint and draw, but not very well.
I just want you to see clearly my story to tell.
It's a tale that's rich and laced with emotion
About how far one will take honour and
devotion.
Its setting so bright, before it gets dark,
Like approaching a quiet dog that starts to
bark.

My tale has a hero, of course a villain as well

One goes through heaven, one goes through
hell
It's got magic and wonder and showers of
dark thunder,
Plenty of treasure to trade, defend or plunder.

If you see my words in your head and my
emotions to feel don't be afraid my world's
not real.
Just take my word for it, do we have a deal?
Ladies and gentlemen and of course the little
ones too,
let's start our tale it begins with you.

90s Kid

Let me tell you a story of some of the things
we did,
Our way of life as a 90s kid.
We did have mobile phones they were the size
of bricks,
We would spend time outside sword fighting
with sticks,
For a weekend movie there was no Netflix,
Just narrowing down your choices in
blockbusters to your top 3 picks.

School was the same,
Just no mobiles to be easily distracted,
If you wanted a conversation,
Face-to-face was how you were contacted,
The best music was taped off the Sunday
radio chart,
Paused and fast forwarded unsure where to
start.

We had viral crazes too that much is for sure,
Marbles, pogs, action figures and so much
more
could be easily found in the Toys R Us store.

But you wouldn't be outside much if you had
an N64.

The Virtual pet on your keys as dead as can
be,
Neglected its attention because there was
cartoons on TV.
Your weekend was done when you heard the
heartbeat theme.
Off to bed of Santa's presents you dream.

This is what it was like for me and countless
others,
I was just lucky to have two older brothers,
they would always look after me if we went
together to play,
Back then I'm sure there were more than 24
hours in a day.

<u>Winter Work</u>

Early mornings in winter the alarm goes off
I toss and turn, "5 more minutes with scoff "
If only I was rich I wouldn't have to work
today
I'd sit at home with my dog and play.

Up out of bed or else I'll be late,
I don't think my colleagues would appreciate
the wait.
Time to shower and maybe feel a little more
awake,
I Hope there's coffee in the pot for the world's
sake.

Now I'm clean and feel a little more alive,
Coffee and toast before my morning work
drive.
Grab my car keys and head out the door,
I wish I was staying home, nothing I want
more.

I head to my car and the sky's still black,
It's too late for a sickie there's no heading
back,

When I drive home the sky will look very
much like night.
5 pm a moon or two ago you couldn't see for
sunlight.

I'll come home when my work shift is done,
It's not all that bad my colleagues make it
fun.
Maybe I will have takeaway for tea,
Maybe not there not exactly free.
Home time now the best part of my day,
I can't wait for springtime,
For winter to go away.

The Best of Luck

My four leaf clover waiting to be found,
My special penny to be picked from the
ground,
A lucky rabbit's foot on the end of my keys
I need some good fortune in my horoscope
please

Tarot cards on the table, clues to what's in
store
Happiness is my drug always searching for
more.
Cards on the table, play where they fall
I just want blessings shining through the
crystal ball

The future can be read if you believe and
understand,
Some people can show you by reading your
hand.

Maybe the future isn't for us to glimpse into,
Fate could bring everything that's meant for
you
I'd rather not know what waits ahead.
What will be will be
Not a truer word said.

An Arrival at Last Chance Saloon

At the end of the dusty trail,
I'm surely beat exhausted and frail,
I fix my hat and walk inside,
I'm sure this place has no rules to abide.

As I enter two men rush past,
Guns in hand, one screams to the other "Let's
make this fast".

A piano in the corner played at a steady pace,
One would almost think if it's the heartbeat
of this place,
Gunshots in the distance, the patrons let out a
cheer,
Not caring for others if they're covered in
spilled beer.

Aces and eights litter the floor, its dry
blood-stained panels,
like the piano playing, hard to ignore.
A waitress emerges with a smile and asks
"What you for, you know I could keep you
company handsome for a few dollars more."

At the end of the bar a stranger dressed in
dark red shouts to the barman.
"Shot of whiskey!
Make it quick or else you are dead,"
With a nervous laugh the barman nodded his
head.

How did it come to this,
The next time I shoot I better not miss,
I'm not looking for trouble or I'll be hanged
by noon,
Waiting for god to help me, In the last chance
saloon.

<u>A Thank You To The Reader</u>

Well we have had,
Cowboys in bars,
And a jewel thief get caught,
A few other stories I enjoyed writing a lot.

This collection started with my four-legged friend,
but there's only one way this book could end.

With My thanks to you for reading my very first
book.
It means the world to me that you stopped to take a
look.
Writing this was really fun and if it's sparked a
thought, feeling or emotion then my job has been
well done.

Much love and kindness
Lewis Kenneth Turner
(Author of From a Fidgety Mind)